MIKE HURT

TECHNICAL BLOGGING

**The Ultimate Guide To Blogging for Beginners,
Learn the Secrets and Strategies on How You Can
Build and Launch Profitable Autopilot Blogs**

Descrierea CIP a Bibliotecii Naționale a României
MIKE HURT
  TECHNICAL BLOGGING. The Ultimate Guide To
Blogging for Beginners, Learn the Secrets and Strategies on
How You Can Build and Launch Profitable Autopilot Blogs /
Mike Hurt. – Bucharest: Editura My Ebook, 2020
  ISBN

MIKE HURT

TECHNICAL BLOGGING

**The Ultimate Guide To Blogging for Beginners,
Learn the Secrets and Strategies on How You Can
Build and Launch Profitable Autopilot Blogs**

My Ebook Publishing House
Bucharest, 2020

TABLE OF CONTENTS

INTRODUCTION AND WHAT YOU WILL LEARN

Making a living as a blogger has to be one of the sweetest gigs out there. As a blogger, you'll be able to earn passive income which means that your money will flow in even as you're sleeping, travelling or relaxing with friends. You're no long trading time for income and this is the point you need to get to if you want to *really* be free and financially independent (even being self-employed with clients is still pretty much like having a job).

What's more, blogging means you get to earn that money by writing on a topic that you find fascinating and you even get to become something of a minor celebrity in your chosen niche. You can earn a lot of money here too - if a blog takes off and becomes really successful then in theory you can earn thousands a day. It's incredibly scalable and there's no 'upper limit' for what you can achieve.

What's the downside? It's not easy. This is all about working hard and smart *now* so that you can reap the benefits later. Too many people approach blogging in the wrong way, thinking that they can just write a few posts on a semi-regular basis and that that will be enough to ensure their success. In reality, you need to approach blogging as a full-time job if you ever want it to be your main source of income. In other words, if you want this to be your full-time job... you better *treat* it like one.

That means working hard and to begin with you want to be uploading as much content as possible, having invested a decent amount of time and/or money in creating a beautiful design to begin with. At the same time though, it also means being *smart* about how you're going to build your blog and it means using growth hacks so that you get much more benefit out of the work you're putting in. Get this right and you can apply force multipliers that will take years off of the time it takes for you to reach number one.

Think that it can't be done? Think that making money from a blog is a one- off fluke that happens once in a blue moon? Think again! The stats really paint a different picture and show blogging to be a *highly* profitable use of your time.

BLOGGING STATISTICS AND WHY

YOU SHOULD CARE

- Marketers who rely on their blogs make 13X more money than those that don't.

- Companies with blogs receive 97% more links inbound to their website

- Blogs are the 5th most trusted source of accurate information online!

- 81% of consumers trust information they get from blogs

- Well over 150 million people in the US alone read blogs regularly

- 23% of internet time is spent on blogs

- 61% of US customers have made purchases through blogs

- It is generally thought that content marketing – AKA blogging – is now more powerful than pure SEO

As you can see then, blogging is very much a force to be reckoned with and there's *more* than enough here to go around. Time to get a piece of the pie!

WHAT YOU WILL LEARN

If you're still reading then you're probably rather excited at the prospect of becoming a 'career blogger' and you probably can't wait to get started and to begin earning money from e-book sales. Fortunately, you happen to be in the right place and this book will serve as your blueprint to ensure that all your work is focused on the right things.

Specifically, by the end of this text, you will have learned…

- How to choose a niche to work in
- How to create a stunning website
- How to work with outsourcers
- How to add advanced features
- How to create content that people will want to read
- How to ensure a steady stream of new posts
- How to hack growth with influencer marketing and other techniques

- How to keep the discipline to keep writing

- How to monetize your site so that you earn the maximum amount from each visitor

- How to use the best tools for bloggers and webmasters

- And much more!

So you have the information laid out for you… there's nothing left to do but start reading it and then begin your journey to Instant Blog Profits!

CHAPTER 1

SELECTING YOUR NICHE

For those not down with the lingo yet, a 'niche' basically means a subject or a topic. This is the area of interest that your website is going to focus on and it's what you'll be writing about on a daily basis for your blog posts.

This might sound like an easy job – but picking your niche is actually something you should consider very carefully. Getting this right can make your life a *lot* easier, while choosing poorly can make it almost impossible to achieve the success you're looking for.

Here we will look at some considerations that you need to bear in mind when picking your niche.

A Topic You Enjoy

Tip number one is to *always* choose a niche that you enjoy reading and writing about. Blogging is not a 'small' job by any stretch of the imagination. Remember when we said it would essentially need to become your full-time career if you wanted to be very successful? Well then you have to ask yourself – is this something you will be happy to write about on a regular basis?

Writing will also come a lot easier if you're well-versed in the subject. You'll need to do less research and at the same time, you'll find it much easier to come up with new interesting topics that people who like the subject will be interested in. What's more, your passion will come across in the content and people will be much more inclined to read more of what you have to say as a result.

Even if you plan on outsourcing your writing, knowing the niche you choose well will help you to feel excited about your site and to check over the accuracy and usefulness of the writing you're receiving. Ultimately, choosing a niche just because some 'guru' says it's a profitable one is a fast track to becoming bored and disillusioned and ultimately giving up.

Popularity

When picking your niche, you need to think about the competition out there and how easy it is going to be to stand out. Of course you want a subject that has a large potential audience, so why not pick something big like 'fitness' or 'cars'?

Well, that's a good idea on the face of it until you think about how many *other* bloggers are writing in those niches. Bodybuilding.com is one of the largest sites on the net and it generates a huge turnover – most of which is invested *back* into the site to ensure a steady flow of new topics. Question is: can you compete with that? Are you going to be able to compete with *any* of those sites to get to page one?

On the other hand, if you choose to blog about rearing stick insects, you'll likely find that there's a much smaller audience – but also far less competition.

The best case scenario then is to find a topic that is popular but that isn't *so* popular that it's going to attract lots of huge companies and top-name bloggers. Things like 'foraging', 'knitting', 'writing', 'parkour' are all big without attracting *too* much attention.

Broad vs Specific Topics

Another strategy is to start with a topic that has a broad appeal but then to narrow it down to something more specific. For instance if you like fitness, how about picking a certain area of fitness such as running or CrossFit?

Or alternatively, what about targeting a particular group? For instance 'fitness for diabetics'. You can also try *combining* two different topics. A great example of this is the blog 'Nerd Fitness'.

Another alternative strategy is to go very *broad* with your chosen niche which has the advantage of allowing you to come up with lots of new angles for content. If you do this though, you risk a lack of focus so you need to ensure that you keep everything tied together with a common thread. A great example of this is the 'Art of Manliness' blog. This blog writes about anything that could be considered 'manly' – so that includes editorials on the role of the modern man but also posts on how to smoke a cigar or enjoy whiskey and posts on how to raise children. This gives a *huge* broad range of topics for the writer while still having a very strong brand identity and focus.

Choosing a Profitable Market

Another consideration when picking your niche is whether or not it's profitable. That's right: some niches are far more profitable than others and you'll find it easier to monetize depending on which one you pick.

Examples of highly profitable niches include finance and business. These are profitable because they offer ROI in themselves: someone will be happier to spend money on an eBook about earning money because in theory they'll make that initial expense back.

Likewise, there is money to be made in any niche that has a big and obvious 'value proposition'. A value proposition can be thought of like an emotional hook – it is the thing that people will want to buy your products or read your blog for and the 'way' that they hope their lives will benefit.

Fitness is a great example because people *badly* want six pack abs and are willing to pay. The same goes for dating.

Monetizing that blog on raising stick insects on the other hand will be harder. There is simply not the same demand or 'need' for products here. That said though, the relative lack of competition in the area, combined with the relative scarcity of information means there are certainly ways to monetize.

Ultimately it's worth just thinking hard whether or not your niche is going to be profitable or not and weighing this up when choosing whether to write about it. Look at your competition to see whether they look to be making much money, think about your business model and maybe even try verifying your intended business model. Verifying means trying to sell to your target audience first to see if they are actually there and if they are actually interested in buying your product.

CHAPTER 2

HOW TO PICK THE RIGHT BLOG PLATFORM

Got your niche? Great! The next thing then is to think about actually setting up your new site and getting started with your content. To do this, you will need to choose a 'blogging platform' which effectively dictates how your site's code will be structured and what you'll see when you're logging in and adding content.

Now of course, you don't actually need a 'blogging platform' as such. You *can* go about building your own website from scratch which will involve creating pages in HTML and CSS, possibly using a builder like 'Dreamweaver' but if you do this it will take a lot longer *and* be much harder to create something that looks and performs like a professional website.

Instead then, you want to use a blogging platform/CMS. CMS stands for 'Content Management System' and is essentially a tool that simplifies the process of designing and building your website, as well as adding and editing content as needed.

Use a CMS and you won't need to know a line of code in order to build the site, to add new posts and to edit your existing content. This of course saves a lot of time, it streamlines the process and it ensures that your site is at least functional.

Choosing Your CMS

So how do you choose a CMS?

The first thing to do is to recognize the difference between hosted and self- hosted options.

A hosted option is a blog platform that you use almost like a social network. In other words, you create your account and 'sign in' to another website and from there, you'll then be able to add new posts for other users to see. In other words, the platform and so your website are *already* hosted somewhere online, meaning you don't need to pay for a hosting account to get started.

Good examples of hosted blogging platforms include: BlogSpot (www.blogspot.com), LiveJournal (www.livejournal.com), WordPress Hosted (www.wordpress.com), Wordpress Self-Hosted (www.wordpress.org) and Tumblr (www.tumblr.com).

Each of them has strengths and weaknesses, though they all do *essentially* the same thing. Tumblr here is really the odd one out as it straddles the line between blogging platform and social media platform – and as it mainly focuses on images that you upload as opposed to written content.

The great thing about this is that it's a completely free process and requires absolutely no set-up. You simply visit the blogging platform, be that BlogSpot or WordPress, sign in and then start posting! You can make changes to your blog in terms of the way it looks but you'll be quite limited in terms of what you can do. Likewise, you'll also be limited in terms of your URL – meaning that you won't be able to call your website 'BodybuildingNewsArticles.com' – instead your blog will have to be 'wordpress.bodybuildingnewsarticles.com' or 'blogspot.bodybuildingnewsarticles.com'. This of course looks far less professional and it also means your URL is going to be far less catchy and brandable. People will likely not remember your URL and type it back into the address bar – they'll have to search on Google. And that said, even searching on Google will be harder seeing as it's not as easy to get hosted websites to 'rank'.

For all these reasons you're much better off with a self-hosted CMS. This means you'll need to pay for the hosting space too as well as a domain name. In all, this will likely set you back $100-$500 for the year but if you monetize well you should be able to make that make even in year one. If you plan on becoming a professional blogger, this is really a mandatory expense.

When it comes to hosted blogging platform options, you have a few popular options. These include:

- WordPress (yes, WordPress is both)
- Joomla
- Drupal

WordPress is available as both a hosted and a self-hosted CMS option. If you go for the hosted option, you will simply need to visit WordPress.com and start an account. If you want to go for a self-hosted choice, you'll instead want to download the install files from WordPress.com, then upload them to your server. You then navigate to one of the files in your browser and the set-up process begins.

Which self-hosted platform should you use? The answer is WordPress *by a long shot*. The reason for this is partly that WordPress is simply the most popular blogging platform. In turn, this means it also has the widest support. That means that you'll be able to find plenty of developers to work with who are well-versed in the platform and it means you'll be able to easily find additional plugins and themes to install to take your site to the next level. We'll look at what themes and plugins are in a moment but for now all you need to know is that they significantly increase the capabilities of your website and are often free to use.

The fact that WordPress began life as a blogging platform also gives it another big advantage. That is that it is highly user friendly and compared with Joomla or Drupal, the control panel is much more accessible and easy to use.

But most of all, you should use WordPress because everyone else does… That might sound like a somewhat lame reason but think about it: most of the most successful bloggers on the net use WordPress. Countless people before you have shown that a WordPress website *can* be incredibly successful… so why then would you use anything else that is much more of an unknown quantity? Why would you take your chances with a more complicated platform? We know that WordPress *can* be optimized for search engines, we know it *can* be very well optimized… if you're serious about making money then it's the logical choice. And the websites created with it look great.

Choosing a Name and URL

As you're going with a self-hosted option for your blog, you'll now need to choose a URL. This is the address that people will type in their search bar in order to find your website and as such it will probably also act as the title of your website and the brand you're going with.

Choosing your name is another very important step here and there are two big factors to consider when making this decision:

- SEO
- Branding

SEO is search engine optimization – in other words, tweaking your website to ensure that it will likely to rank highly on Google and to show up in searches. Your URL affects your SEO because some URLs are much more 'searchable' than others and this will give you an edge over the competition.

In other words, if you wanted to rank highly for our earlier example – bodybuilding news articles – then having an address like bodybuildingnewsarticles.com or bodybuilding-news-articles.com would be a great advantage. This won't *guarantee* you'll rank highly mind and those who have done more work at their SEO could still beat you in other ways – it's just a good head-start and advantage.

In terms of branding, you want to choose a URL that is the same as, or similar to, the name of your website. So a business called 'Spination' would do very well to get 'Spination.com'. Again, this isn't a requirement but it will make several things easier – not to mention promoting your site and making it more memorable.

If you don't have a site name yet, then this is a good time to think about it. Aim for something that's unique and interesting, catchy and at the same time descriptive. In a perfect scenario your URL will tell people what your site is about without just being a boring description. So in reality, 'bodybuildingnewsarticles.com' is a dull URL that's not great for branding. Much better would be something like BroNews, BBNews or MuscleTalk.

This is easier for creating logos, for making an impression and more but it still will give you *some* SEO benefit and won't be too obtuse.

As for your 'TLD' or 'Top Level Domain' (the 'com' or 'co.uk' part), it's still always preferable to aim for the '.com' if you can. An exception to this is if you're running a local blog in which case a regional TLD is better. In most cases though, '.com' is the easiest to remember and thus the simplest to promote.

CHAPTER 3

HOW TO CUSTOMIZE YOUR BLOG'S APPEARANCE

From this point on we shall presume that you are using WordPress. If this is not the case, then most of the following advice will apply but some of the specifics and details may be different.

Now that you have your URL and you've installed WordPress, you're ready to start creating. The first thing to do? Think about the design you want to use!

But that doesn't mean your *web* design. This won't come until later. Instead, you're going to focus on your logo first. Why? Because your logo is a crucial part of your branding and chances are that you're going to want to use a web design heavily inspired by your logo. Your web design will probably use colors from your logo, it will probably use certain visual cues and this will help to create a consistent design language for your entire site. It's a great starting point and it will make coming up with your design that much easier.

Creating a Logo

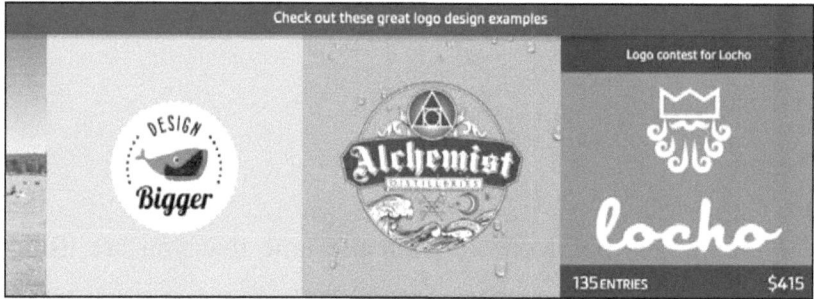

So how do you come up with your logo? The first stage is to recognize what makes a good logo. Critical criteria here then are:

- Versatility
- Simplicity
- Originality
- Suitability

It needs to be versatile and simple because you're going to be using this in various different places throughout your online presence. Your logo will go right at the top of your website but it's also going to go front and center on your Facebook page, it will be right up top on your Twitter page. And if you build an app then it will be there too. We'll see later how important it is to have a strong presence on social media: and having a great logo will really make a big difference to that and will help to create brand visibility and loyalty.

In terms of originality, you need to avoid obvious clichés that are present in too many logos. Ticks, globes and lightbulbs have been done to death and as such you should really avoid these unless you want your website to look like a massive cliché.

That said though, don't go for something so creative that it doesn't communicate your message at all. Your logo should entirely on its own tell visitors what your site is about and what type of site they're on. This will tell you whether the logo should be fun, whether it should be professional and whether it should be colorful.

To take a look at some logo design samples that meet the criterias described, go to 99designs:

http://99designs.com.au/logo-design

The Process

A great process to go through when creating your logo is to create a mood board. This is essentially a collage where you will place everything that you can think of that you like, that relates to your business and niche and that you might consider emulating. This can be other logos, it can be photos of color palettes or it can be random sketches you've made. Create a big enough collection and eventually you should find that some themes and patterns begin to emerge. This way you can then start sketching some ideas, combining elements and trying out different approaches. Some you will like and some you'll throw out. This spit-balling process though will help to lead you in the right direction.

Likewise, it can help to look at the name of your website and brand and to try working with that. Are there any letters that could be morphed into one of your related items? What should the font look like?

For text, it's important to use an interesting font that looks professional. Ideally, you'll also want to use a font that is unique to you. A good solution here then is to download a custom font from FontSquirrel.com (a great repository of free TTF and OTF files) and then to *trace over* your company name, making edits as you do to make it original. This way, your font will be unique but at the same time, it will be based on something that looks professional.

Finally, take whatever you have designed and then simplify it and scale it back. Remove anything superfluous and the more you cut away, the better and more impactful it will be.

Note that when you create your logo, you should do so using vector software. This includes the likes of Adobe Illustrator. Vector software works differently from raster software that produces PNG and JPG images. While the latter creates a 'map' of where all the pixels are going to go, the former lets you define the angle, length and direction of the lines that create the image. This means that vector images can be drawn at any size with no loss in quality and that you can easily make edits to the image when you need to use the logo in a new context. The best choice if you can afford it, is to use Adobe Illustrator. This will produce an AI file and you can then use that to make new PNGs as they're needed.

Choosing Your Theme

Now you have your logo, you should have some ideas for your color palette and you should be ready to start thinking about the artistic direction of your website.

At this point, with WordPress installed, you should already have a rather attractive looking website that utilizes WordPress' default theme for the year. The current 'Twenty Fifteen' theme looks very sleek and modern with light colors and a very 'picture heavy' layout.

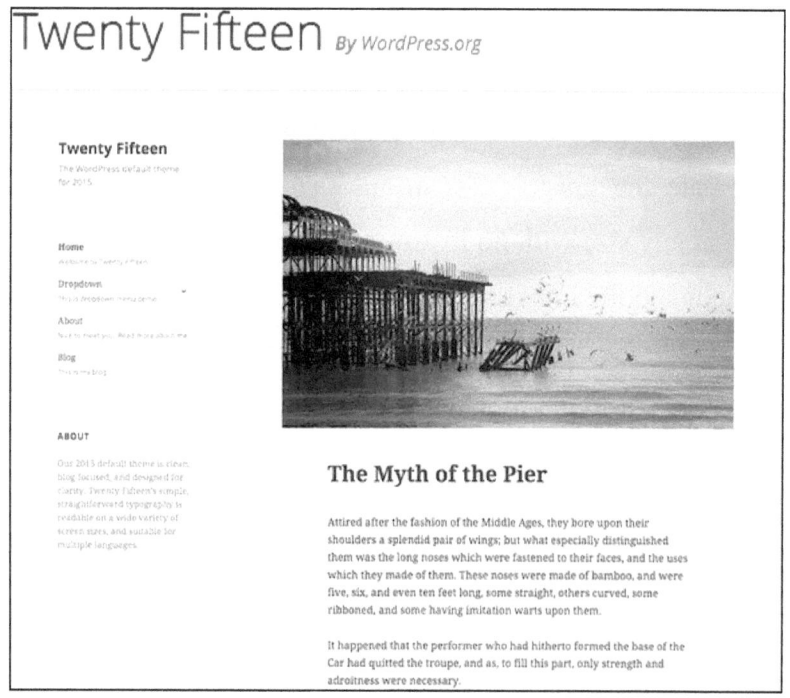

You can swap the title for your new logo and right away you'll see that it looks out of place. It's also important to use a theme as otherwise your site won't look very professional – it will look as though you didn't know *how* to create a theme of your own and so opted to go with what was available by default.

Adding a theme means applying a new layout and look that has been predefined for you. This can then instantly change the visual impact your website makes, as well as the way your visitors will navigate around it.

You can find themes to install for free right through WordPress and can preview them through the control panel before selecting which one you want. The problem with free themes though is that they tend to be less professional looking than paid themes and they tend to have fewer options. At the same time, there's always the risk with a free theme that someone else will have chosen exactly the same theme of you. This dilutes your brand identity and it doesn't exactly scream professionalism.

Instead then, it might be better to look for paid WordPress themes. This can again be done through your WordPress control panel, it can be done by looking on other sites like Theme Forest, or it can be done by hiring a team of designers to create a custom theme on your behalf. Of course that latter option is the best way to get a theme that is perfectly matched to your branding and your requirements.

When choosing a theme, try to keep a few things in mind. For starters, you need to pick a theme that will be well suited to the type of website you're going to create. Some themes are very image-heavy for instance and will feature sliders on the front page as well as lots of large crisp images linking to each of the posts you upload. This is a great way to make your blog look more modern and more visually compelling but at the same time, it's also important that you consider the work that goes into this and the requirements. Will your content lend itself to being image heavy? Will you have the means and resources to acquire lots of large graphics that you have the rights to use legally? Do you want to spend time reshaping the content?

Certain themes will also be well suited to sites with lots of content and will have large menus for finding your way around. Other themes on the other hand will be better suited to sites that are made up of a single or a few static pages.

You should also look for some specific requirements for your theme, no matter what type of blog you're looking to create. Make sure that:

- The theme is responsive, meaning it looks good on any sized display

- The theme is optimized for mobile in other ways – for instance, the buttons should be large enough to be pressed with a finger instead of a mouse click

- The theme is quick to load so that people don't get bored and leave and so that Google doesn't penalize you

- The theme *looks* good and professional and is easy to navigate

If you're torn between themes, try taking a look at some of the blogs that you enjoy and admire. What layouts do they feature? What is good or bad about that? Again – if they've *shown* that that kind of layout can work, it basically verifies the strategy and ensures you won't be wasting your time working with a doomed web design.

A great place to look for premium themes you can buy is at ThemeForest.com.

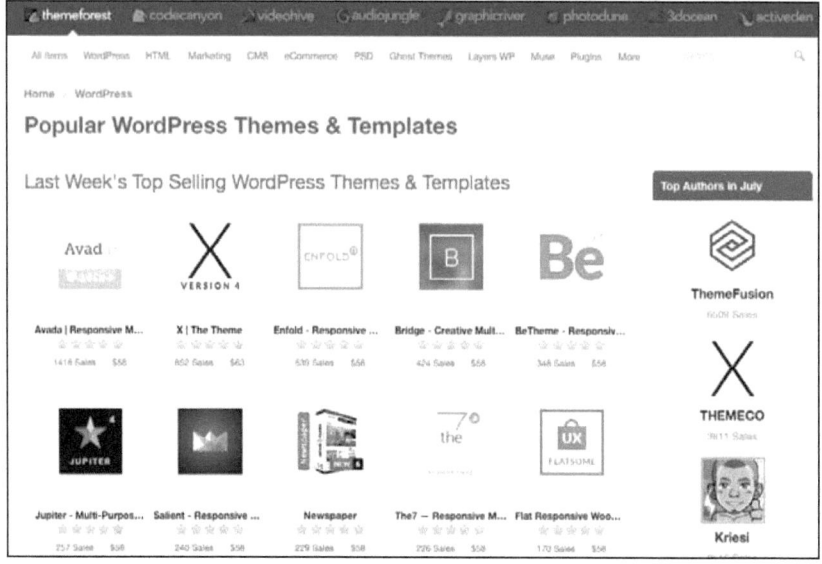

Customizing Your Theme

WordPress is *highly* customizable and this is another one of its huge advantages. We've already picked a website theme but now we can go one step further by tweaking that theme to be just the way we want it.

WordPress allows you to do this by default under the 'Appearance' tab where you can change things like your header and footer, your logo, your background, the color scheme etc. Most themes though will also come with their *own* options panel where you can make additional tweaks and customizations.

One thing you should do right away is to match elements of your website to your logo's *precise* color code. This will create a strong sense of consistency throughout your web design and will ensure that everything matches neatly. It's not enough to feature 'almost the same' blue – it needs to be 100% identical blue.

A few recommended and popular Wordpress themes you can use are Thesis (http://diythemes.com/) and the Genesis Framework (http://my.studiopress.com/themes/).

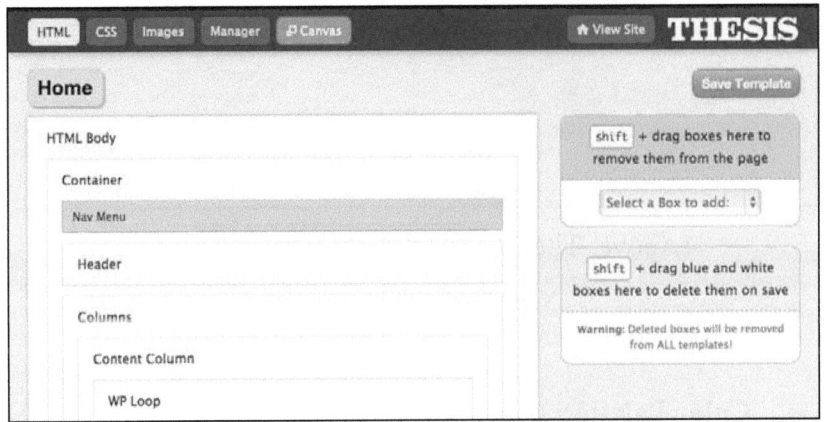

(Above: The Thesis theme editor)

(Above: The Genesis Framework - a popular
Wordpress framework)

Color Palette

At the same time, think about the other colors on your
website. One way to do this is by applying a little 'color theory'.
Color theory basically tells us which colors should look good
together and which shouldn't on a color wheel.

When using this approach you have a number of options. One is to pick 'complementary colors' which are the colors opposite each other on a color wheel. Purple and green look good together for instance as do any combination of three colors spaced evenly apart. Another option is to go for 'analogous' colors which are colors that are directly next to each other on the color chart.

Finally, you can also pick 'natural' color schemes. These are color palettes that you select from photos in nature: looking at photos of natural scenery and picking out the colors that occur heavily in those.

Make sure to think about practicality as you do all this. Just because a color scheme looks good, that doesn't make it appropriate for a website. Ask: is it easy to read?

To get help with finding your colors, try going to Pintrest and search for "color palette". You'll find images of colors you can combine.

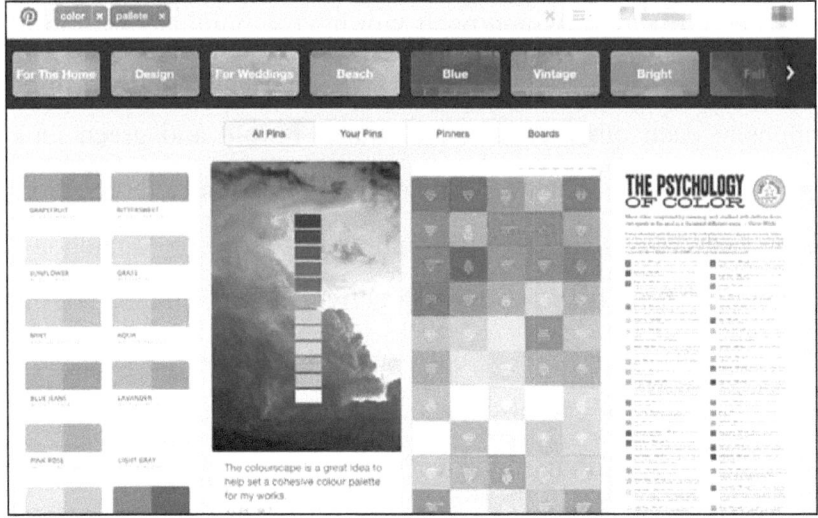

Fonts

Another consideration is your choice of fonts. This is a relatively small detail in the wider context of your web design but it's actually small details like this that make a web design look professional and give it that 'sheen'.

Don't just work with the fonts that came with your theme then: think about adding new typefaces that will be easy to read on a range of devices and that will complement the tone and topic of your blog.

For instance, a 'serif' font is a font with the small feet at the ends. More often we use 'sans-serif' (no feet) fonts on the web because it's generally easier to read and it looks very crisp, minimal and modern. But if your blog is going to be reporting news, or if it's literary in nature then you might want to consider using a serif font. Why? Because serif fonts have been traditionally used in print mediums and as such they have become associated with that kind of niche.

Combining fonts can also be used to good effect. For your headings and titles for instance you might opt to pick something bolder and larger without worrying as much about legibility.

Choosing a Background

Adding a custom background can also do a lot to customize the look of your theme and this is something you can update yourself relatively easily. Again, pick something that is on-point as far as your niche goes and which will add to the look and feel of the site.

Adding Widgets

Another way to customize your WordPress theme is by adding widgets to the sidebars. Widgets are small forms, sidebars and other elements that can provide all kinds of functions on your site. For instance, many 'opt-in' forms for mailing lists will take the form of widgets, as will many advertising slots, feeds from social media etc. Using widgets is a great way to give your site more features and you can add additional widgets by installing them as plugins.

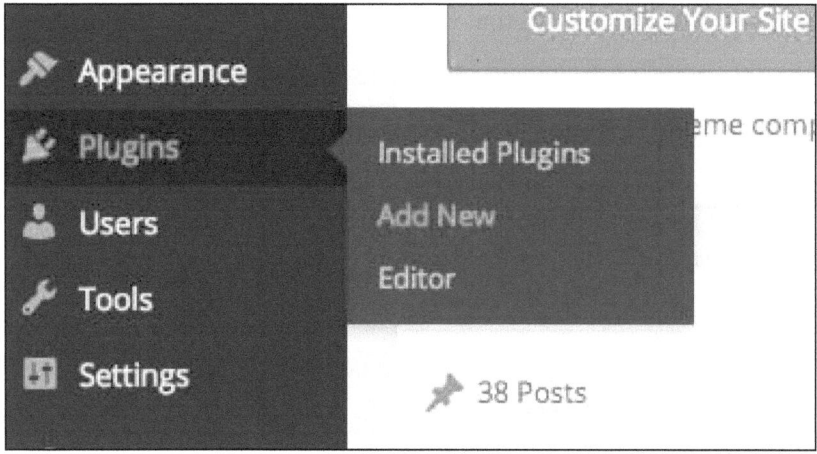

Just go to Plugins – then add new plugins to find widgets and 'behind the scenes' tools that will enhance your site's performance in all manner of ways.

Outsourcing

If all this is sounding rather complicated then there is an easier way – which is to try finding an a company you can outsource the work to. A great way to do this is to visit a freelancing site where freelancers can post their CVs and you can post your job offers.

Good freelancing sites include UpWork (www.upwork.com), Elance (www.elance.com), Freelancer (www.freelancer.com) and even Fiverr (www.fiverr.com). You can also just look online for agencies offering web design and WordPress skills. For logo specific work, I recommend 99Designs (www.99designs.com).

CHAPTER 4

HOW TO WRITE AND CREATE
KILLER BLOG CONTENT

Having a beautiful site with nothing on it is not enough though. If you want to start growing your visitors and building momentum for your new business then you're going to need to add *content*.

Why 'Content is King'

Content generally refers to 'writing' when used online and in the case of a blog this means blog posts. This type of content is what most of us are looking for when we search for things on Google: we want information, entertainment or opinion. Thus, by adding more content to your site, you give people an incentive to visit and you let yourself get to know them.

Content is important for more reasons that that though. For instance, it also happens to be your site's content that will ensure you win or lose at SEO. Search engines work by trying to match search terms to the content on a website. The more writing you have, the more chance there is of you getting a 'hit' and the more people will start finding your site with relevant good queries.

Content is also critical for 'content marketing'. Content marketing is basically a form of marketing that revolves around your blog posts. The idea here is that you're going to update your site regularly with interesting articles and posts and this should then help you to find genuine *fans* of your work. These people might subscribe to your site, join your mailing list (more on that later) or just bookmark your page. They'll then come back regularly to see what interesting new content you've added lately and each time they do, you'll have a new opportunity to market to them.

What's more, content marketing will allow you to demonstrate your knowledge and expertise on a subject. If your readers get to the point where they respect what you have to say and they start seeking you out for answers to questions, then you'll be able to sell to them more easily when you recommend an informational product you've made, or perhaps an affiliate product you're getting commission on.

Content is also crucial for your social media marketing (as you can share it to your channels to get more followers) and it can be used to sell things directly. In short, the success of your blog revolves almost entirely around the content that you'll be uploading to it.

How Much Content Should You Be Adding?

So here's the golden question: how much content do you need to add to turn your website into a big success?

There's no single answer here though and of course the best guidelines will depend on what your blog is about, who your typical reader is etc. You should also keep in mind that quality always trumps quantity.

BUT the simple guideline for how much content to add is just: as much as you possibly can while staying consistent.

Consistency is key.

We've seen all the ways that content can help your website. We've seen that 'content is king' and that SEO basically amounts to adding writing to your site for Google to find... and with that in mind, it follows that the more content you can add, the more chances you will give people to find you and the more you'll stand to make from your site.

We touched on this briefly in the introduction already but this is really the key point you should take from this e-book. To be successful from a blog, you need to really invest yourself in it. That means spending a *lot* of time making tons of great quality content and then promoting it. You can upload a blog post once a week and be fairly successful. But if you want to skyrocket yourself to prominence you really need to be posting multiple times a week or even multiple times a day. Your rewards will grow exponentially the more top-quality content you are putting out.

How Many Words Should Each Blog Post Be?

Now that you have an idea as to how much content you should be adding, the question now is how many words or length should each blog post be?

According to Neil Patel of QuickSprout.com and statistics from SerpIQ, longer posts are usually better.

Typically longer posts attract more search traffic. Take a look at this graph from SerpIQ:

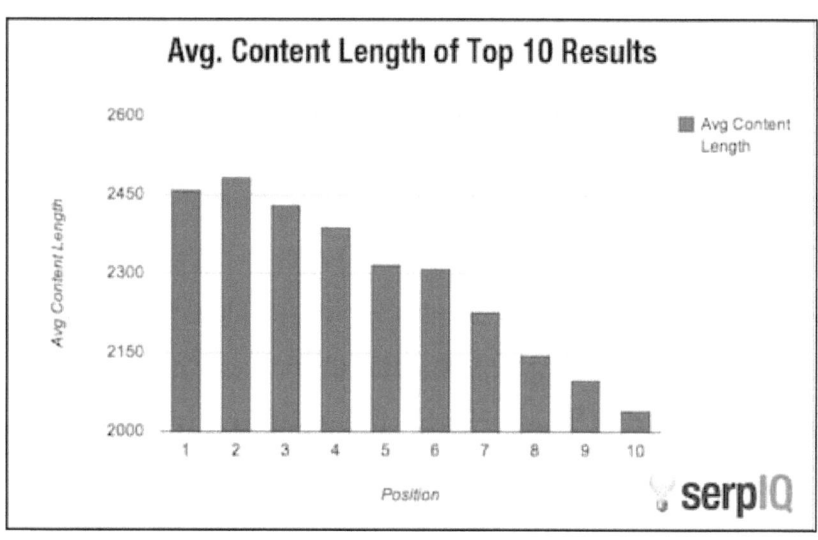

Notice the top content length is sitting around 2000 words.

Longer posts are usually more comprehensive than a short 500-word article--there's more meat and detail in it.

Why it's better for search traffic is because you are including more h1, h2, h3 headings and keywords within your posts.

The higher your word count, the more link-backs you'll get. Take these graphics from Moz as proof:

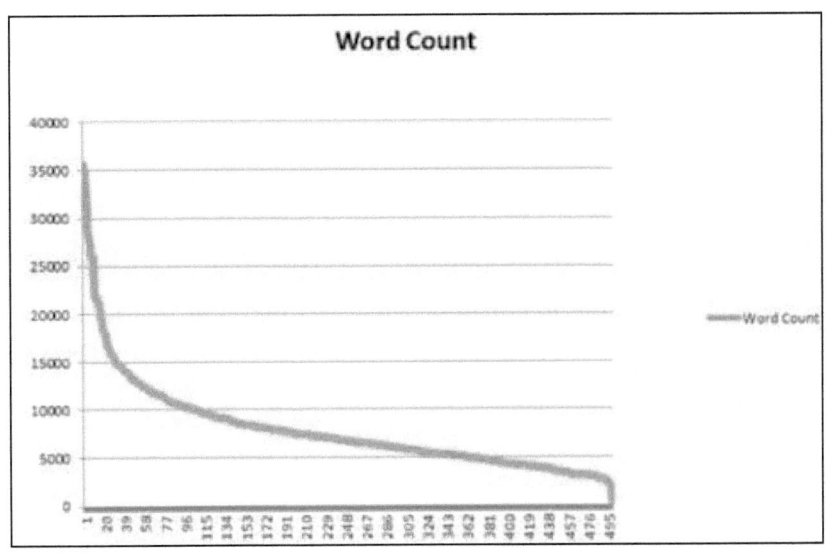

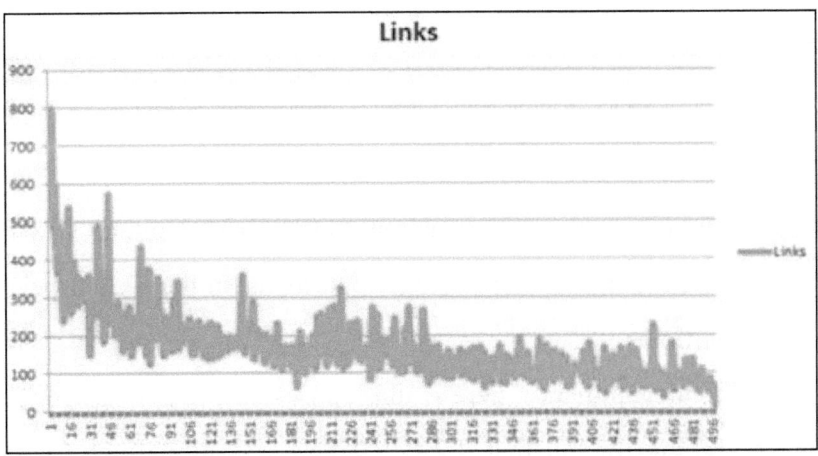

More link-backs means more search traffic. Neil Patel says:

"My own research on Quick Sprout confirms this. All of my posts that are more than 1,500 words receive 68% more tweets and 22% more Facebook likes than the articles with fewer than 1,500 words."

Just something to consider when writing your posts.

Choosing Topics

The next question then is how you're going to go about picking topics to write about. How do you bring something fresh to your chosen niche that hasn't been seen before? How do you ensure that your content is going to bring in readers and that it's in demand?

SEO

I shared some tips on search traffic earlier but let's talk about it a little more. One strategy is to focus on the SEO aspect of your articles.

The ideal situation here is that you write a post that people are searching for but that doesn't yet exist. Alternatively, you can try and write a subject that is popular right now but not yet over saturated.

You can do this by using keyword research tools. Keyword research tools effectively allow you to see what people are looking for and how the competition stacks up.

The best known keyword tool is Google's own 'Keyword Planner' (http://adwords.google.com/keywordplanner).

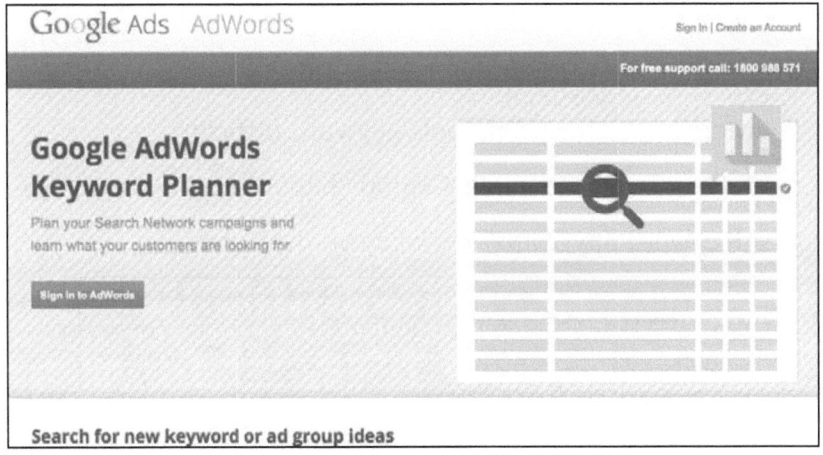

This is designed for people who are thinking of using Google's paid 'AdWords' platform for advertising and the idea is to show which search terms might be a good use of investment capital for a company hoping to gain exposure to a specific audience. Unfortunately though, Google 'depowered'

their keywordplanner a while back because they didn't want to provide too much information for those trying to 'game' their search ranking system. This means that you can't see all of the good keywords currently available.

Instead then, you might decide to look into alternate options like the free Wordpot, or paid Moz Keyword Analysis, Raven Tools Research Central or Keyword Spy.

Links to each tool:

Wordpot: https://addons.mozilla.org/en-us/firefox/addon/wordpot-the- keyword-finder/

Moz: https://moz.com/tools/keyword-difficulty

Raven Tools Research Central: http://raventools.com/seo-tools/ Keyword Spy: http://www.keywordspy.com/

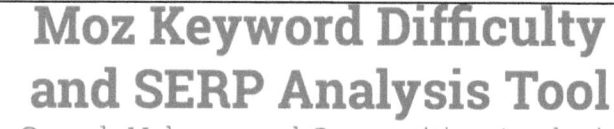

Moz Keyword Difficulty and SERP Analysis Tool

Search Volume and Competitive Analysis for any Keyword or Phrase

Choose the right keywords to minimize your time and effort, and maximize your results.

To use these, simply search for the topic of relevant terms alongside the search volume (how many people are regularly searching for them). From there, you can then try searching the term yourself in Google and then seeing what the competition looks like. Find a highly competitive keyword, then ask yourself: can you do better than that? And also: how?

For added SEO benefit, you then want to subtly lace your keywords into the content, so that you are occasionally repeating the phrase in a non-forced manner (as well as using related terms). Don't make it obvious (this is called 'keyword stuffing' and it will get you penalized) but just take the opportunities as they arise.

Keyword research is a very handy tool for finding topics that will be a hit for your website but make sure that you don't let keywords dictate the topics of your articles – otherwise you'll end up with a bunch of generic posts that are written for Google *over* actual humans that might read them!

Places to Research

Another way to get great ideas for content is simply to keep an eye on what other people are talking about and on news. Looking at forums in your niche is a great way to do this, as you can see what people are talking about, asking questions about etc. You can even post there yourself and just ask what people want to hear more of!

Of course you can also look at what your competitors are writing about and you can look at news sites. News sites generally have sections like health, technology etc. and these can provide useful topical prompts for your content. Note though that anything that is too topical will not be 'evergreen'. In other words, it will have a limited shelf-life as far as being relevant goes which means you won't be able to get more value out of it in future.

Another trick is to look at news from websites *not* in your niche and then to *combine* that news. In other words, you might have a fitness website but perhaps a new motion-controlled computer game is relevant? Or maybe you could write something based on technology?

Easy Ways to Get Content

Looking to get content without having to put in all the leg work yourself? As it happens, there are a number of ways you can get good content for 'free' and without working.

One is to create 'curated content'. Curated content is simply content that you have gathered from around the web. None of it is original but by collecting it all in one place, you can offer something new.

A very basic example of curated content would be a list of famous or inspirational quotes for instance. You can go further than that though and use full paragraphs, links or even entire short articles. As long as you are providing value to your target audience by collecting all the content into one place, it will be useful for your readers.

Note as well though, that curated content runs the risk of penalization from Google. Google doesn't like people to use 'duplicate content' which is any content that has already been published elsewhere. Of course your curated content runs the risk of falling into that trap. This is fine: just make sure that you drive most of your traffic to this particular article from social media and try to avoid using this strategy too regularly. Another tip is to use smaller passages – this can also help you to avoid being guilty of simple copypasta.

Another way you can get great quality content for free is by publishing the work of guest bloggers. Guest bloggers are bloggers who publish content on your site in exchange for a free link back to their site. This gives them some promotion and you get some free content in the process – it's a genuine win/win scenario!

CHAPTER 5

HOW TO ADD VIDEO AND IMAGES TO YOUR BLOG FOR MORE ENGAGEMENT

Due to its considerable SEO advantages, text should always be the main source of content for your website. However, with that said there are other types of content you can choose form too. For instance, videos have a number of advantages in that they're high engaging, very memorable and very persuasive. Images meanwhile will really help to sell your content and especially when people see previews of it on social media sites.

How To Add A Video To Your Blog

The easiest way to add video content to your website is to create a vlog on YouTube (a video-log or video-blog) and then to embed it onto your pages as posts. Always make sure to write a little content underneath too as this will help you to rank on those pages.

More importantly though, having video built-in to your blog will give visitors another in-road to reach you. This way, you can use video marketing through YouTube and build up a list of subscribers there to introduce to your website.

Meanwhile, you'll be able to get your blog subscribers to check out your YouTube channel and connect with you that way too. This is the first real example we've looked at at creating synergy across web channels and it's a very powerful strategy if you're interested in gaining more exposure for your content. Again, make sure you have a strong brand here which will really help to tie everything together. Show your logo in your video opener, have it as a watermark on your video and use it on your YouTube channel page too.

Having videos on your site will also give your visitors the chance to get to know you (assuming you're going in front of the camera). This also shouldn't be underestimated as it's a highly effective way to build a 'personal brand' which is often even more memorable than a more corporate brand.

To add a video, simply get the link to your video and paste it into your post. If you are using Wordpress, it will automatically convert your video into an embedded video.

Step 1: Copy the URL

Step 2: Paste into your post

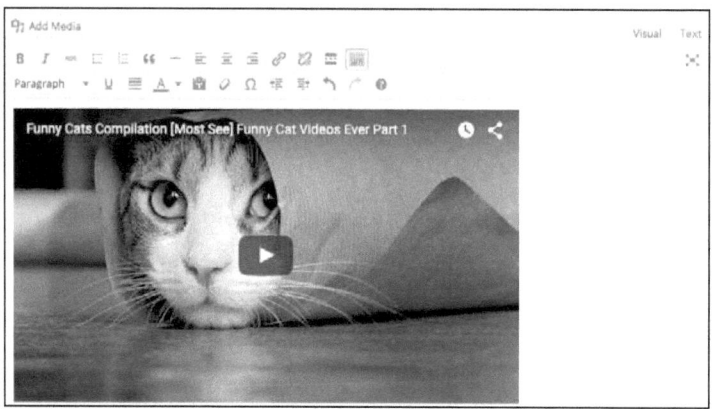

Adding Images

Adding images meanwhile can help to break up long passages of text and to greatly heighten share ability. When you post links to articles on your blog to Facebook or Google+, bear in mind that the title and the image are the only two things that will encourage people to click or not. This is one of your most powerful assets then and it's critical that you use both wisely.

The right image should not only attract the attention of social media users but should also communicate what your post is about and why they should read it. Some people will even 'like' or share content before they've even read it if the image is convincing enough!

Of course you can make your own images by taking photos or by using editing software but often you'll be able to save time *and* ensure a professional quality by using stock photo sites instead that provide you with free images that you have the rights to use. There are many such sites but good examples include http://morguefile.com and http://depositphotos.com.

You can also search Google Images and other image sharing sites to find photos that you can use. To do this though, make sure that you have selected 'labeled for reuse' or 'labeled for reuse with modification' if you plan to make changes. This way, the image *should* come with a creative commons license meaning that you are permitted to use it on your site and even to profit.

CHAPTER 6

HOW TO PROFIT FROM YOUR BLOG

With everything you've learned so far you should now have what it takes to be a successful blogger, insofar as you know how to create a blog and then grow it to the point where it's getting tons of traffic. But while this is highly rewarding, it's not going to give you the freedom that you're looking for.

This will not be enough to enable you to quit your day job and to start lying in in the mornings/spending more time with your family/travelling.

To do *that* you're going to also need to monetize your blog – in other words ensure that it's bringing in cash.

So how do you do that? The answer might surprise you…

Consider This Before You Spend A Single Cent On Advertising

Many people believe that the best way to make money from a website is by putting ads on it – specifically like Google AdSense that will pay out every time they get clicked (this is 'PPC' advertising meaning 'pay per click').

Simply sign up for an account at https://www.google.com/adsense, create your campaigns, paste the adverts you create onto your site to embed them in your content and then ensure that lots of people are going to your site.

Problem is though, you're only going to earn a few cents per click from those ads. If you're getting hundreds of thousands of views per day, then this can be a good way to earn a fair amount of passive income – but even then there are smarter and more effective ways you could be earning *more*.

The thing to keep in mind here is that those advertisers are willing to pay you that much for your traffic. What this tells you, is that the customers are worth more to them than the small amount they're paying you. That means they must have found a *better* way to monetize their site – likely by selling a product or perhaps an affiliate product that they'll gain commission for.

Either way, this now means that you're selling something for less than it's worth. How do you get to the top of the pile?

Creating and Selling Products

The very best way to make money from a blog is to sell something. You can do this by purchasing inventory in bulk and then selling it on for more than you paid for it but this is a rather involved and complicated process with a number of challenges.

What's much easier then and what's particularly well suited to blogging, is to sell an *informational* product. That means an e-book, a book, a digital course or something else.

(Above: an information product created by DigitalMarketer.com)

As a digital product, these options will have zero overheads for you and no delivery costs. What's more, you'll be able to demonstrate value and build trust in your product through your content marketing very effectively. Throw in some adverts for your product and some promotion within the body of your content and you can make a lot of money this way.

Note that if you aren't confident enough or don't have the time to write an entire e-book, you can always outsource the process using the likes of UpWork (www.upwork.com), Freelancer (www.freelancer.com) and Elance (www.elance.com).

Affiliate Marketing

Or if you'd rather not invest the time or money in creating products, another choice is to skip that part and instead sell someone *else's* product. You can do this by becoming an affiliate marketer, meaning that you're now selling a product for commission. If that sounds like a step-down from selling your own product, bear in mind it gives you a much wider selection of things to sell and that it means you can choose products that are *already* highly successful.

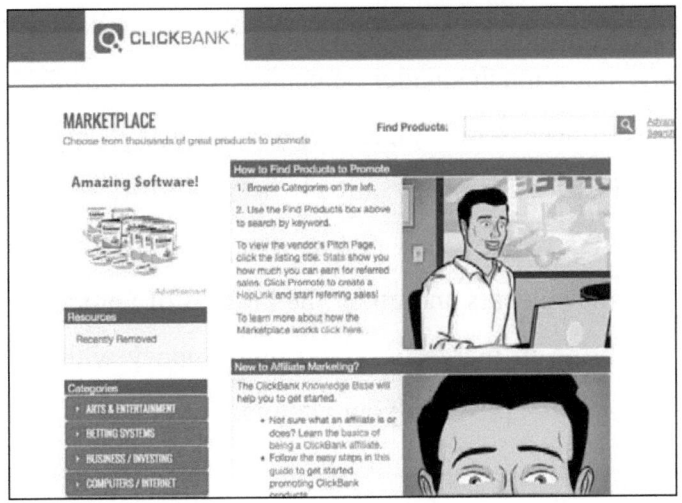

If you find an affiliate product through a site like ClickBank (www.clickbank.com) or JVZoo (www.jvzoo.com), you'll be given an affiliate link to promote and every time someone clicks on that link and buys the product you'll get around 40-60%. A great strategy then is to include product reviews as blog posts, or to have a list of 'key resources' for your readers that promote these items.

Another option is to choose Amazon's affiliate scheme. This pays out a much smaller percentage but on the other hand, it gives you access to a gigantic selection and it lets you sell through a retailer that people already use and trust.

Look for widgets and plugins that will let you add your adverts in the sidebars and under the headers of your site. These key spots bring in more clicks and more money without being distracting or disruptive for your visitors.

You can use a plugin like "Amazon Product in a Post Plugin" to add formatted Amazon products to any page or posts. It's free: https://wordpress.org/plugins/amazon-product-in-a-post-plugin/

CHAPTER 7

BUILDING AN E-MAIL LIST

Think of your website as a sieve. Most of the people who visit it will read it, enjoy it but then fall through the tiny holes never to be seen again. At this point they are lost.

This is why e-mail marketing is so important. With e-mail marketing, the objective is to get visitors to sign up for a mailing list so that you can update them with news about your new posts, new products and more. This lets you turn a one-off visitor into a loyal fan and someone you can reach regularly. Don't rely on RSS feeds for this kind of loyalty – it's only a small selection of people who use these and barely *anyone* will subscribe to an RSS feed on Feedly on their very first visit.

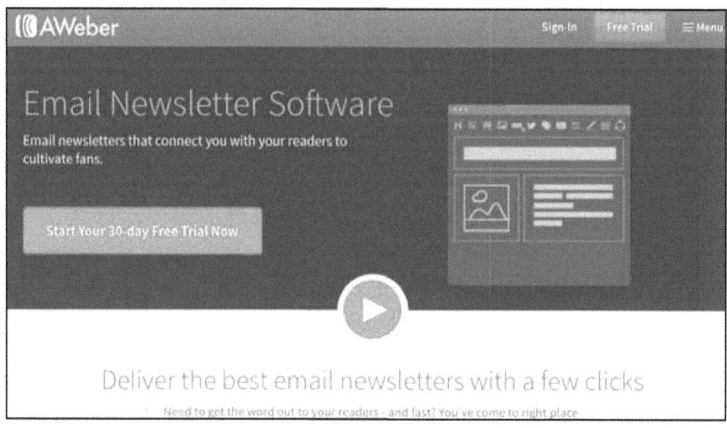

To create a successful mailing list, you will need to use an autoresponder along the lines of Aweber (www.aweber.com) or GetResponse (www.getresponse.com). These will manage your contacts, allow you to send large bulk e-mails and also automate the process of signing up or unsubscribing.

Once you've chosen a platform and signed up, you'll then be given the opportunity to create an 'opt-in form'. This is where your visitors will enter their details if they want to sign in and it's what you should work to promote if you want to get the maximum visitors possible.

Fortunately, it's relatively easy to insert opt-in forms into your sidebar and into the bottom of your posts. This won't be enough to encourage first time viewers though: if you want to go the extra mile to secure subscribers (which you really should) then you should incentivize your mailing list with an e-book, a free report or some other kind of freebie.

Likewise, you can put your opt-in form into a lightbox that appears over the rest of your content. SumoMe (www.sumome.com) is one example of a useful 'pop-up' lightbox you can use to convert your one-time visitors into subscribers and long-time customers.

Now make sure you keep your mailing list active by notifying your members of new updates to the blog and by mentioning your offers and promotions.

Note that pretty much *every* major blogger describes their mailing list as one of the absolutely crucial aspects of their business model. Don't ignore this!

CHAPTER 8

SOCIALIZING YOUR BLOG

Post regularly enough and your blog will begin to generate 'long tail' keywords and will get traffic from Google. You can help this as well by exchanging guest posts and submitting your links to directories and forums to create a big 'in-bound links profile'.

In this day and age though and especially for bloggers looking to build a personal brand, social media is going to be your very best tool for promoting your site. This will allow you to directly reach your target demographic, to engage with your audience and to grow your list of fans and followers.

So how do you go about effectively 'socializing' that blog?

The Basics

The first rule of social media is 'be everywhere'. This means you should have an account on Facebook, on Twitter, on

Instagram (which is actually bigger than Twitter!), on Google+, on LinkedIn... you name it! And across all these accounts you should have a consistent logo, a consistent brand name and a consistent mission statement and niche. This will help to give people more ways to discover you and it will present more ways to share your content.

Now when you post your blog posts, you should also share them to all these channels. As you gain more visitors, more people will gravitate towards your social media. And as *they* grow in number, the content you share there will automatically start to perform better.

At the same time, you should also think of sharing your links to social sharing sites – like Reddit (www.reddit.com) and StumbleUpon (www.stumbleupon.com). Also good are Facebook groups and Google+ communities. This way you can find specific audiences for your content who will be likely to enjoy your content and to share it and promote it.

In fact, every time you write a new post for your blog you should have a good idea of all the ways you can share it socially. Where will this be the biggest hit? Who precisely are you aiming this post at? Think of your route to market right from the start and you'll all but guarantee succeed.

Of course you should also add social sharing buttons right *into* your content. You can do this with a plugin like Shareaholic (www.shareaholic.com). This lets your visitors share your content with their contacts if they should enjoy it.

Creating a Community on Your Own Blog

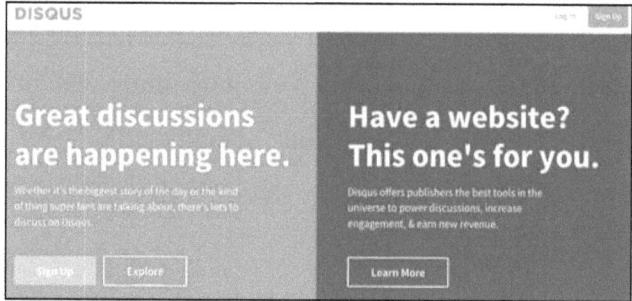

Another smart tip is to try turning your own blog into a community itself. You can do this with an active comments section (use the plugin in Disqus which has a lot of advanced features and useful advantages) and by just making sure that you always respond to comments and generally encourage conversation. Try to end your posts with an invitation for people to discuss more – or even end them with a question.

And do take the time wherever possible to answer e-mails, messages on LinkedIn etc. Don't underestimate the value of a single highly loyal fan!

CHAPTER 9

IMPORTANT PAGES TO HAVE ON YOUR BLOG

As well as posting content as blog posts, a WordPress site also lets you add pages. These will be static points of interest on your site that people will be able to view regularly whenever they're interested in them.

This chapter will serve as a useful reference for adding pages to your blog...

About Page

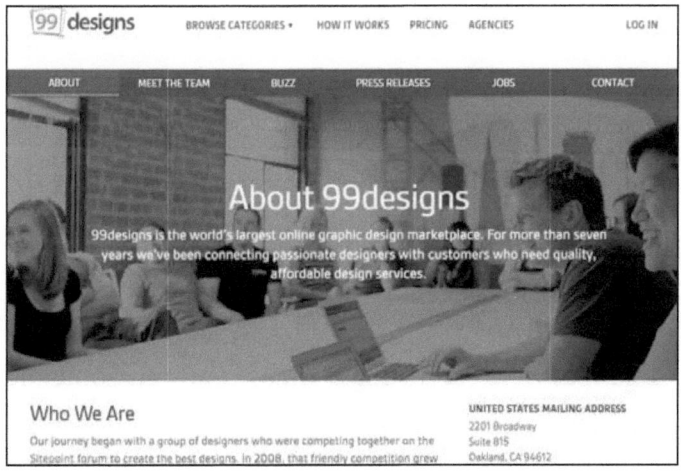

An About Page is a page where you tell people about your blog. This is an excellent opportunity to explain your mission statement and to help new visitors make sense of everything they see on the home page. If you have lots of content, this can help you to tie a little bow around it all and to get people excited for your future output. You can also use this to weed out your 'non audience'. In other words, to really hone in on your specific target demographic.

Contact Page

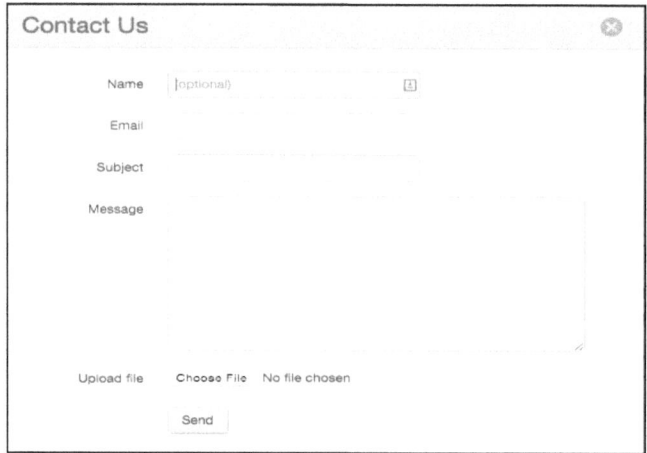

For gaining fans and for building new contacts and networking opportunities, a contact page is an absolute must. Leave this out and you might miss out on some serious opportunities!

A good way to let people get in contact without opening yourself up for abuse is to use 'Contact Form 7' (https://wordpress.org/plugins/contact- form-7/).

Just another contact form plugin. Simple but flexible.

Download Version 4.2.2

Description Installation FAQ Screenshots Changelog Stats Support Reviews Developers

This is a plugin that adds a form to your contact page and helps protect you from spam.

Services

This is another great way to monetize your site! Why not turn some of that expertise into a service you can charge top dollar for?

Products

This is where you will promote your own products or your affiliate products. Some bloggers will call this page something like their 'essential gear' or their 'survival kit' and for real fans it's a great place for people to gain some of your magic for themselves.

Recommendations/Resources

This is similar to the above but will work more purely for affiliate links. What products can you unreservedly recommend?

Here is a screenshot of a blog using a 'Resources' page:

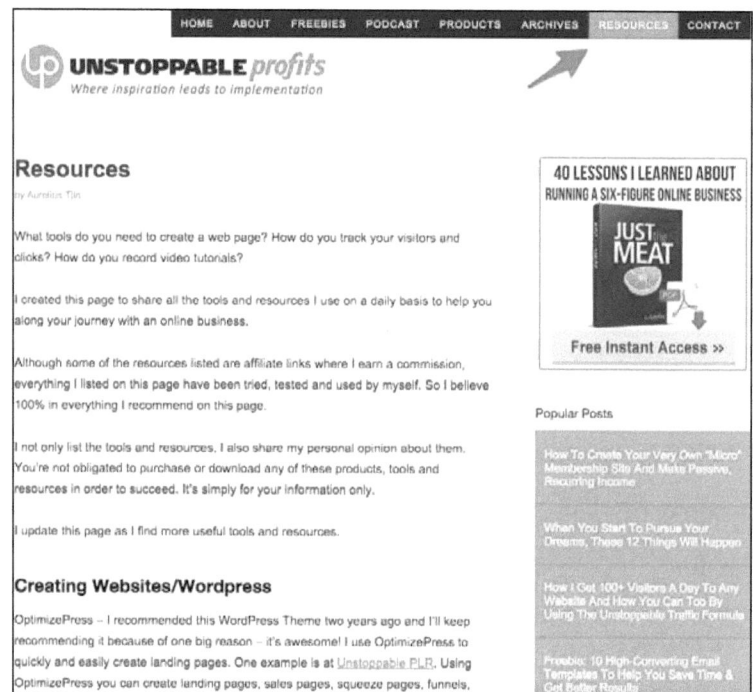

'Start Here'

The only downside with the blog format for websites is that it can be hard to find older, legacy posts and content. A good way around this is to have a handy 'Start Here' page that can act as a 'jumping on point' for your new visitors and show off the highlights of your site.

CHAPTER 10

CONCLUSION AND THE NEXT STEP

At this point you should now have a rather steady flow of income with a well-designed blog, a consistent brand and loads of unique content. You know how to share it, how to build fans and how to use some of the best tools to save yourself time.

The rest comes down to luck. So just keep plugging away and eventually you'll get your break when your link ends up on the right website or gets recommended by the right person. The key is to *not give up*.

The Next Level – More Blogs?

But once you've started to gain traffic and the money starts flowing in, what can you do to scale your business and speed things up?

One option is to take on a new blog project... or maybe two! This way you can increase the amount of ads you've published, the amount of content, the amount of products you're selling... and at the same time you'll be far more resilient should anything ever happen to your main site (you know what they say about eggs and baskets...).

Choose a niche that is *somewhat* related to your current one and that way you can benefit from some of the momentum your brand will have obtained at this point. That way, you can promote synergy across your different channels and the success of each blog will help to further the success of each of the others.

Don't take on more than you can chew though. If taking up a new blog is likely to mean that your *current* blog doesn't get the attention it deserves, then you should reconsider.

If you're like many people, then you'll likely start out running a blog as a side hustle to bring in some extra income on top of your main job and just for fun. You'll need to commit as much time to it as possible but if you *do*, then you'll eventually be able to quit your job and start living entirely off the blog (though it may be tough at first). *This* would be a great point at which to take on a new blogging project and to branch out and grow.

What We've Learned

So what have we learned throughout the course of this e-book? Before you go on your way to start blogging, remember some of these key pointers to ensure your success...

- Choosing your niche carefully is very important. Pick one that is something you're very passionate about and that is potentially profitable. Avoid overly vague and crowded topics.

- You will need a blogging platform/CMS. The best choice by far is to go with a self-hosted WordPress site.

- Choose a logo and a name for your site next. This will help you when choosing your domain and will inform your web design.

- Web design is easy on WordPress – it's simply a matter of selecting a theme and potentially tweaking it.

- Consider font and color palette at this point. This is highly important: small touches make your site look professional which is what will win you the trust of your visitors.

- If you struggle, hire a professional through UpWork, Elance or Freelancer.

- Add regular content that is high quality. Increase quantity as much as possible.

- Research ideas by using news sites, forums in your niche and keyword research tools.

- But focus on making your articles *interesting*.

- Have in mind an audience for each post you make and know where you're going to share it.

- Sharing to social media is key – ensure a consistent brand identity across all platforms.

- Also share to social bookmarking sites and online communities. Tailor make your content for these audiences.

- Add an e-mail list and use this to bring visitors back to your site.

- Don't monetize with PPC ads – sell a product or an affiliate product.

And there you have it! If you focus on these tips and then just put in the work, you'll eventually find that you can build enough followers to start making a living from it.

Don't get disheartened if this success doesn't come at first – as we've said countless times you really need to invest the time if you want to make this your actual living. If you're writing about something interesting though and you're doing it well, you'll find that you *eventually* find the fans and you actually don't even *need* that many visitors to be relatively successful.

Worst case scenario, you make a few hundred extra dollars a month. Not something to turn your nose up at! If you're truly passionate about your niche too, you should find that none of it ever feels like work.

And it will all be worth it in the end. Imagine being a rich internet celebrity who can travel the world making money from a blog… And imagine knowing that you achieved your freedom through your own hard work and effort! You can get there, you just need to stick with it.

IMPORTANT: To help you further take action, print out a copy of the *Checklist* and *Mindmap* I provided. You'll also find a Resource Cheat Sheet with valuable sites, posts and articles that I recommend you go through.

Printed by Libri Plureos GmbH in Hamburg,
Germany

9 786069 836552